Ethnographic Terminalia: San Francisco 2012
Audible Observatories
SOMArts

© Ethnographic Terminalia, 2014

Published by the Society for Visual Anthropology, a section of the
American Anthropological Association. 2300 Clarendon Blvd.,
Suite 1301. Arlington, VA 22201

Edited by Ethnographic Terminalia:
Craig Campbell, Kate Hennessy, Fiona P. McDonald, Trudi Lynn Smith,
Stephanie Takaragawa

Lead editors and print design: Kate Hennessy and Rachel Topham

Exhibition Photography: Lara Rosenoff-Gauvin

Cover Design: Ethnographic Terminalia, Rachel Topham and
Ian Kirkpatrick

ISBN 978-1-931303-45-3

Ethnographic Terminalia

San Francisco 2012:

Audible Observatories

SOMArts

2012 Principal Curators
Stephanie Takaragawa
Craig Campbell

Local Organizer
Thor Anderson

Co-curators
Kate Hennessy
Fiona P. McDonald
Trudi Lynn Smith

Exhibition Assistant
Calvin Johns

Volunteer
Julie Conquest

General installation view, San Francisco, 2012

Acknowledgements

The *Audible Observatories* exhibition benefitted from the generous assistance, expertise and support from many groups and individuals. Thor Anderson provided significant on-the-ground help as our local organizer and partner for this exhibition. The *Audible Observatories* exhibition was strengthened by the addition of works submitted by Thor's students from San Francisco Art Institute as the projects provided additional local context for the exhibition. The Distributed Exhibition that took place all over the Bay area benefited from numerous individuals and organizations who welcomed our site-specific pop-up exhibitions, these include the LGBT Community Center, Siete Potentias Africanas Gallery, Yerba Buena Gardens, San Francisco Art Institute, and San Francisco Planning and Urban Research (SPUR). Thank you to Alley Cat books who hosted John Wynne's work, Anspayaxw. Jessica Eley worked tirelessly supporting the installation, opening, and de-installation of the exhibition and served as the 'voice of sanity.' Eben Kirksey added an additional scholarly dimension and new audience to the exhibition with his Multispecies roundtable. The assistance of Mary Molly Mulaney and Ed Varga at SOMArts was essential in allowing for exciting active and interactive spaces. We would also like to thank Chapman University students Eileen Regullano, Clay Thomas and Samantha Cressey and University of Texas student Calvin Johns for their assistance in the installation (and planning). We would like to acknowledge the financial and in-kind support from the American Anthropological Association, The Society for Visual Anthropology, University of Texas at Austin (Anthropology), Chapman University (Sociology), Layar and SOMArts.

We would like to express our sincere appreciation to all of the artists who provided documentation for us to review. Finally, we would like to thank the artists in Ethnographic Terminalia both for their work and for their participation.

AUDIBLE
OBSERVATORIES

San Francisco 2012:

Audible Observatories

Ethnographic Terminalia is an initiative that brings artists and anthropologists together to engage emerging research through installation and exhibition. The exhibition acts as a platform for the articulation of divergent modes and methodologies and inquiry, a place to explore what lies within and beyond disciplinary territories, and how their boundaries shape the representation of cultural practice.

Audible Observatories are points of sensory convergence. They are nodes where worlds perceived through the senses intersect and begin the labour of transforming independent events into knowable and meaningful claims. They speak and they are spoken to. *Audible Observatories* brings together works that draw attention to both the situation and the agency of the observer.
The curators for *Audible Observatories* make a playful connection between research-based art and place-bound exhibition in order to animate a curatorial vision that foregrounds audio-centric art works within a broader rubric of site-specificity. We conceptualize the audible observatory as either a mobile or a stationary site of perception that is sensible to others just as it is a place from which sensing the world happens. The relationship between listening and being heard is central to the audible observatory; it is meant to be a relentlessly self-reflexive site of communication in which location-specificity is central in its aesthetic.

General installation view, San Francisco, 2012

General installation view, San Francisco, 2012

General installation view, San Francisco, 2012

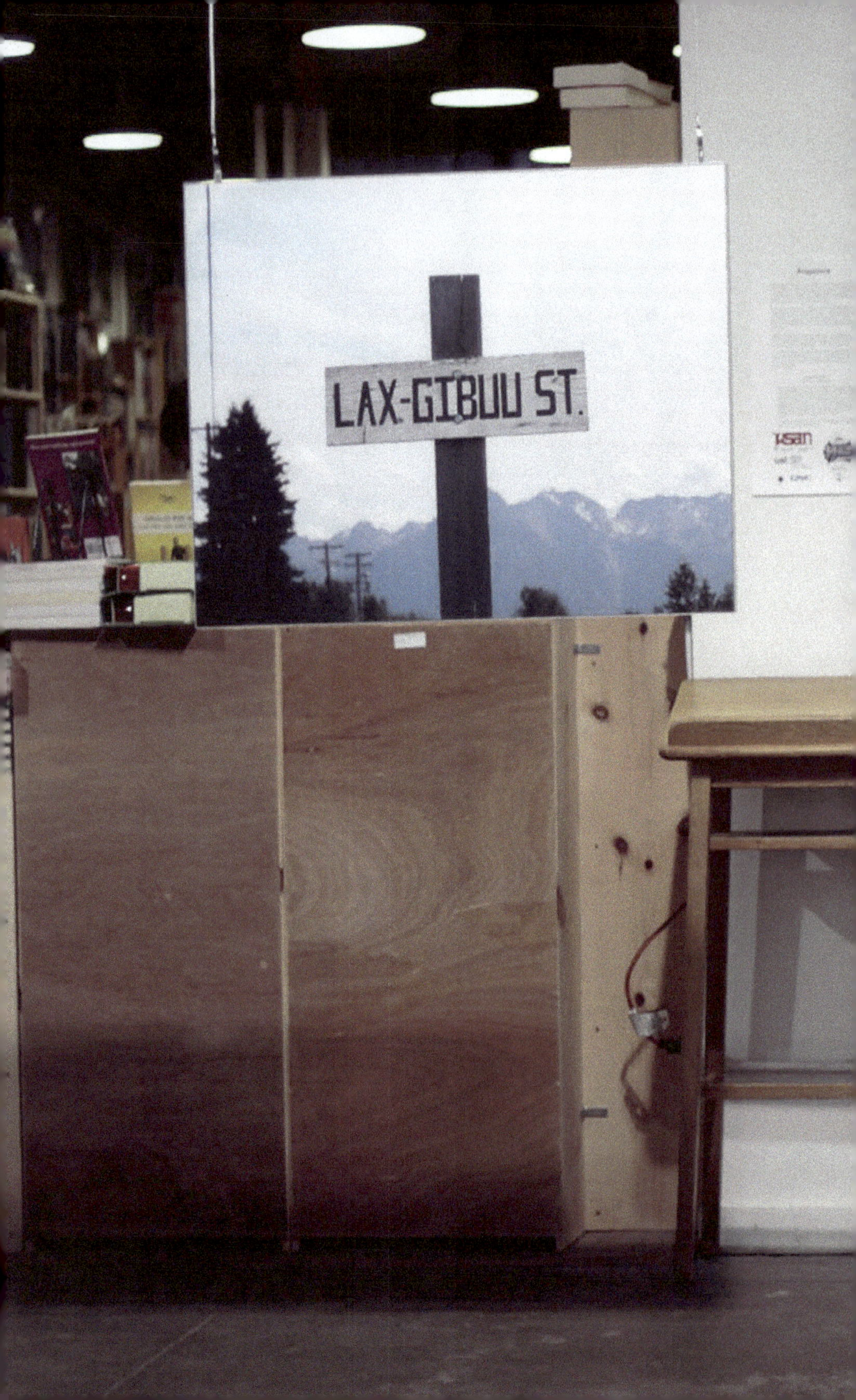
LAX-GIBUU ST.

General installation view, San Francisco, 2012

General installation view, San Francisco, 2012

Amber Ablett
Aural Archive
interactive voice recordings
2012

If our identity is constructed through our past and our memories
of it, the photo albums that we collect act as evidence of the life
we have lived, people we have met, and places we have been. These
act as triggers to our memories and document what we have seen.
Aural Archive is an album of people's voices, collected as a tool of
rememberence. The phrase "fusion, err, pull, woo, each, joy, dock,
whet, young, thou, thaw, vie, ash, home, say, big" uses all of the
phonetic sounds in the English language and was originally developed
for use with audio recognition software. This on-going project will
involve inviting participants and the audience to add their voices to the
archive.

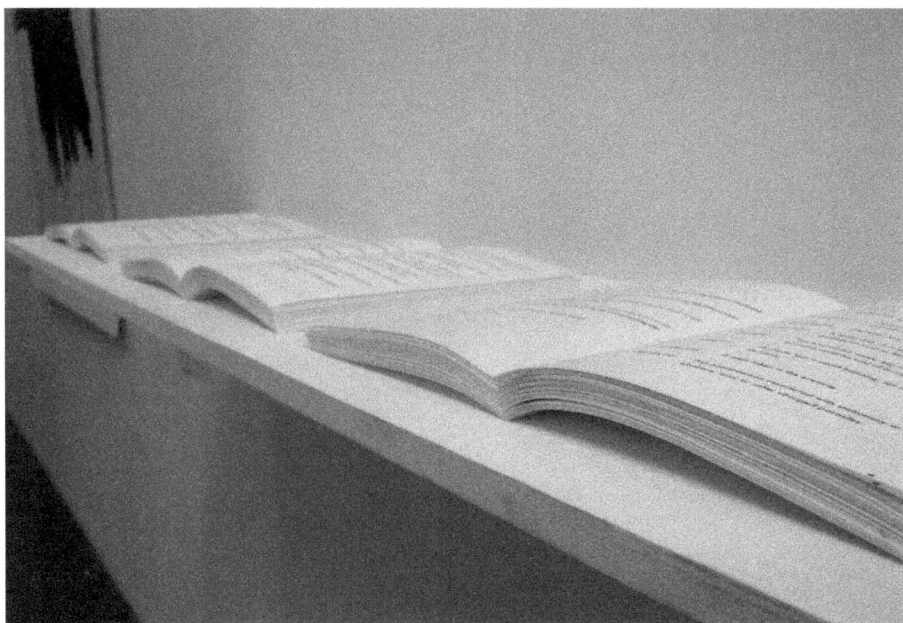

Alejandro Acierto
stolen synthesis, no. 5
projected text
2009

Drawing from theories and positions within critical race and ethnic studies, critical pedagogy, and sound studies, my work is situated in a critical and conceptual framework exploring themes of ambiguity, liminality, and memory that become part of a larger political project to think through notions of fluid identities and the slippages of cultural definitions. Recently, as with this project, my work is sound-based and experiential, inviting viewers and listeners to engage with the work beyond casual observation. This particular work, *stolen synthesis no. 5* deals with the negotiated spaces of mixed-race people who struggle with language learning and reading comprehension as a result of their multi-lingual experiences. While working at the interstices of sound-based art, conceptual art practices, and research-based methodologies of learning, this work highlights the experiences of many multi-lingual people whose identities are almost always called into question. By complicating the ways in which language is presented and "performed", this work disorients and confuses speakers of English by breaking down a question into an 8-minute stream of letters. This slow presentation of text is then further complicated by the addition of a second projection of the same text offset by a minute, creating seemingly nonsensical combinations of letters that further confuse and engage the viewers. Through this exploration of an "imagined sound" (engaged viewers attempt to spell out the letters into coherent words and conventional sentence structures, "hearing" words formulate in their heads), this piece reconfigures one's relationship to sound within a space and begins to ask questions such as, "What are you listening to?", "What are you listening for?", and even, "Are you listening?"
Through this work (and work similar to it), I wish to foreground the experiences of historically marginalized people by highlighting those particular moments of negotiation and subject the viewers to confront them on their own terms. By placing the viewers into these spaces of negotiation, I hope to open a space in which their privileges, positions, and assumptions get called into question.

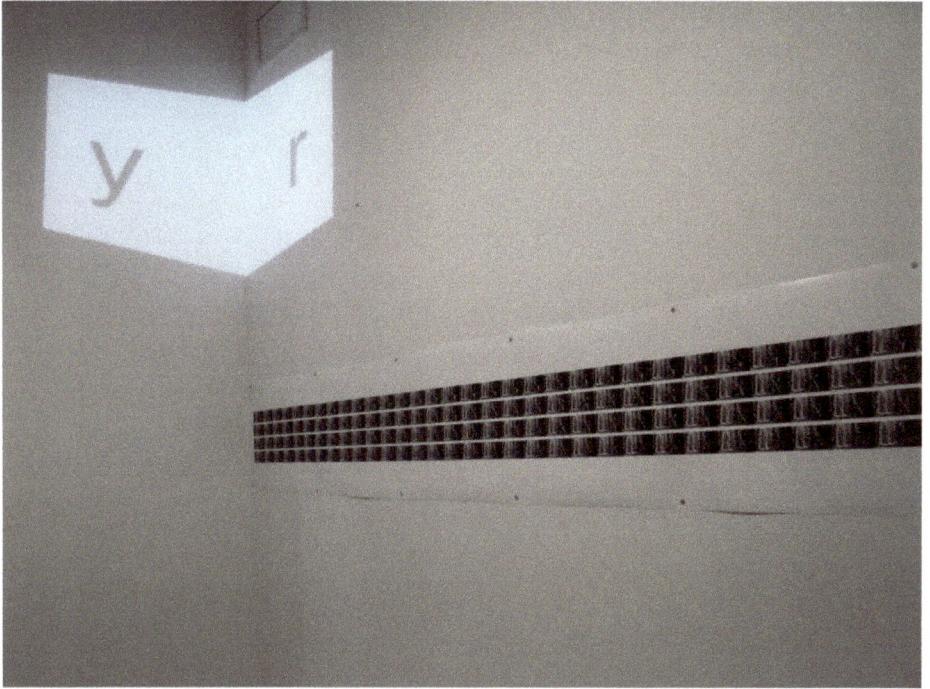

Kevin Allen
Bridge
super-8mm, 11 minutes
2012

A study of three similar but distinct microcultures: the Manhattan Bridge, Brooklyn Bridge, and Williamsburg Bridge. Interrogated through the use of contact microphones, the physical infrastructures of these bridges become audible and reveal their inherent macroacoustics. The film treats the bridge as an anthropological body for discourse, as a physiology of limbs, organs, eyes, and ears moving in time.

Patricia Alvarez
Sintiendo el Tejido / Sensing the Woven
installation: alpaca fibers and garments, with audio landscape
2012

Our current system of supply chain capitalism often creates a
disconnect between the consumption and production of objects.
Consumers do not readily associate objects of consumption with their
socio-economic and production histories. This installation seeks to
explore and challenge this disconnect by inviting a tactile engagement
with an object of consumption via the physical and aural components
related to its making. This piece aims to create a sense of intimacy
between production and consumption processes as well as to reflect on
the interiority, materiality, and social composition of an object.
This collaborative installation is based on 20 months of ethnographic
fieldwork carried out in Peru. During this time, I followed the
growing supply chain of alpaca garments. This supply chain articulates
traditional textile techniques and herding practices with global fashion
styles. As the fiber travels from the highlands to Lima and abroad,
its brings together Quechua speaking herders and artisans, fashion
designers, and development workers into emerging dialogues necessary
to produce these objects. Central to these encounters are the textures
of the fiber and the unmistakable acoustic landscapes of herds, artisanal
workshops, and fashion arenas.

The installation consists of three alpaca objects at different stages in the
production process: sheared fiber turning into thread, an unfinished
garment, and the completed garment. The objects featured in the
installation were made possible through a collaboraton between
a Quechua tejedora (weaver), a Peruvian fashion designer, an
anthropologist, and a computer engineer. This created an interesting
dialogue across actors from diverse social spaces reflecting upon the

look and feel of the objects and modes of interacting with them. As participants interact with the objects they will activate touch-based sensors that enable an audio landscape of the environment where the particular stage of production takes place: alpaca herding space, artisanal workshop, and the boutique/runway. This experience will be mobilized through the immediacy of touch and the audio landscape that envelops the social interactions that make the existence of these garments possible. Through the interaction of object, sound and touch this piece seeks to emphasize the ways in which we are not only audible observers but actors in the world constantly modifying and being modified by objects.

Justin Armstrong
Everywhere is Nowhere
film & audio
2012

Everywhere Is Nowhere is the result of over 2 years of ethnographic
fieldwork in the rural hinterlands of Saskatchewan, North Dakota,
Wyoming, and South Dakota. The images in the film describe the
presence of absence that infects these places, the aura of 'lives-once-
lived' that hovers in apparent emptiness. The audio portion of the piece
is composed of various electronically processed field recordings and a
narrative from Linda Whitney, the last person to live in Sanger, North
Dakota, a town that now lies completely abandoned. This film seeks
to unpack the human inscriptions on deserted space and excavate the
hidden worlds that appear for an instant and then quietly vanish into
the realm of spectral geographies. By juxtaposing images of people-less
places with Whitney's stories of deep inhabitation, this piece attempts to
illuminate the invisible histories of North America's ghost towns. Part
ethnography, part half-remembered dream, *Everywhere Is Nowhere* asks
how places live, fade and die in the absence of human agents.

Alison Ballard
Her Noise Archive, Symbol of Democracy or Communist Uprising?
dual video
2012

Her Noise Archive, Symbol of Democracy or Communist Uprising?, is a
short video work created in response to the Her Noise Archive; an
archive of women working at the intersection of sound, art, noise and
politics.

It considers the distinction between what constitutes political criticism
and rebellion within sound arts practice. It is a sardonic observation
of the ambivalent political voice of the *Her Noise Archive* which serves
equally as a democratic symbol of equality and, simultaneously, as an
uprising against the false utopia of democracy. By presenting both
truths side-by-side the stark similarities between these two viewpoints
are made apparent and its political fragility laid bare. An archive
may be created democratically but it can easily become bound to an
authoritarian existence by those who control its access, changing its
political locale overnight.

Her Noise Archive, Symbol of Democracy or Communist Uprising? extends
beyond critique and passes question upon political party structures
and the fine line between one party's politics and another. Applying
the same structure and techniques of manipulating rhythm, pitch and
repetition I explore the possibilities of speech as a political tool within
the arts.

Amanda Belantara
Ears Are Dazzled
experimental documentary
2012

Created during a 70-day artist-in-residence period at the Akiyoshidai
International Arts Village, *Ears Are Dazzled* is a collective exploration
of sonic experience. Inspired by research addressing the role of sound
in everyday life and its applications for gaining a deeper understanding
of human experience, the experimental documentary was made in
collaboration with locals in Yamaguchi, Japan. I asked them to keep
sound diaries in which they recorded sounds that were relevant to their
daily experiences. We then recorded the sounds and images together,
creating a shared sonic encounter.

Karin Bolender
Gut Sounds Lullaby
audio installation
2012

"Gut Sounds" is a term with significant resonances in American ass husbandry. Listening for gut sounds, or gut motility, is one of the first and foremost diagnostic tools in equine veterinary practice, where the presence or absence of normal gurglings in a donkey's or horse's insides can carry big epistemological, emotional, and economic implications. Indeed, the return of good gut sounds to a beloved equine who's been sick can make those otherwise vaguely obscene inner gurglings seem like the sweetest melodies on earth. On another and more common level of experience, these thrumming, rhythmic, and liquid sounds of digestive and circulatory inner workings are the first ones we all hear as mammals, as our ears begin to function with months to go in utero and our brains mesh with the sounds of the world, throbbing through the permeable boundaries of our mothers' bodies.

The *Gut Sounds Lullaby* installation frames layered sites where gut-sounds phenomena fold in with questions of presence and invisibility in forms of intraspecies being-together. Odd to think that gut sounds are something we seldom attend to, even as their presence signals life and cessation equates to death. Living gut sounds surprise us with their immediacy, bubbling up bigger questions of bodies' unknowns, along with the ways we manufacture ontologies through the boundaries we draw between inside/outside, human/animal, and self /other. *Gut Sounds Lullaby* seeks to blur some of these boundaries, pressing our ears to their seams to listen for what hums on the other side. We invite listeners into the presence of an intricate and intimate auditory mesh, where real-time equine gut sounds are wired into and amplified by the layered resonances of improvisational electronic music/sound collage and an invisible but present human fetus, who we presume will be listening on the other end of the intraspecies transmission wires.

Rupert Cox and Angus Carlyle
Air Pressure
audio and video
2011

Air Pressure is a collaboration between anthropologist Rupert Cox,
sound artist Angus Carlyle, and the acoustic scientist Kozo Hiramatsu.
The sound-film *Ki-atsu: the sound of the sky being torn* shown here
is part of the *Air Pressure* project, which explores the clash between
traditional farming life in Japan and the technology and economy of an
international airport through the sounds generated by their everyday life.
It uses sound recordings, as well as on-site and archive film, to represent
the sonic experiences of living and working on a farm that is surrounded
by the airport's infrastructure and constantly monitored by surveillance
and sound measuring mechanisms.

Two remaining farming families – of the estimated 360 who arrived
after WWII – still live at the end of the runway at Narita International
Airport in Japan. This project follows one family, the Shimamuras, who
refused to move elsewhere despite pressure from the authorities. The
original farming community of Sanrizuka had spent 20 years turning
cedar forest and scrub into productive arable land, the fertility of the soil
derived from the weathering of volcanic ash sent up by the eruptions
of Mt. Fuji. In 1966, the Japanese Government set about securing the
Sanrizuka farming land in order to build what was then called the
New Tokyo International Airport. A bitter struggle played out over
the next 12 years until the airport opened in May 1978. Farmers and
their supporters built tunnel complexes, "fortress towers," and chained
themselves to trees. The police used water cannons, baton charges, and at
one point more than 200 construction vehicles in an effort to clear the
site. There were deaths on both sides.

Air Pressure is primarily based around two periods of field work in
Japan, one scheduled to coincide with the harvest in 2010 and one
coinciding with the sowing season of 2011. All the recordings were
made on the site of the Shimamura farm, a family who continues to
make their livelihood from an organic small-holding with fields of

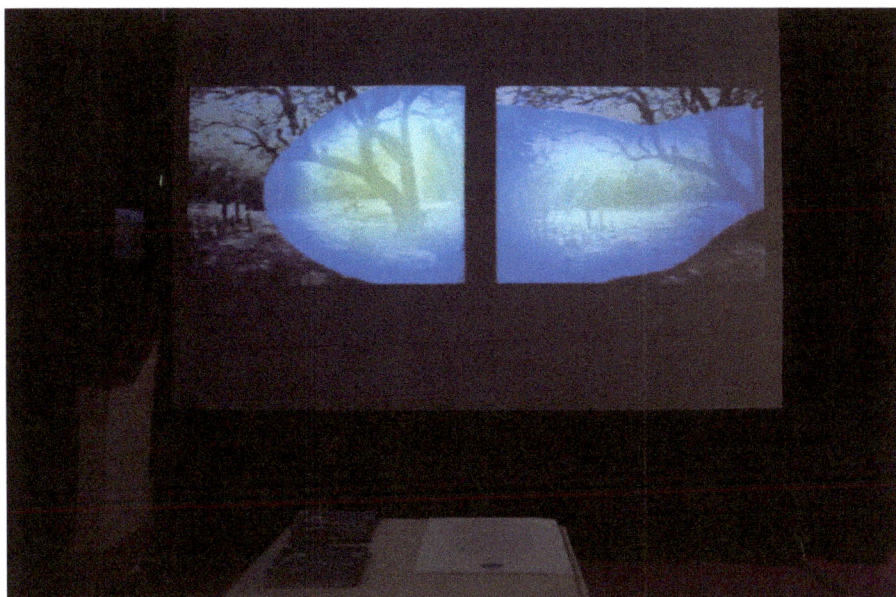

fruit and vegetables, pens of pigs, and a barn with egg-laying hens. The farm where we lived and worked is almost completely engulfed by the architecture of the airport. More than this, the environment is frequently submerged beneath the blurring din of taxiing jets, a din that is punctuated by the roaring descent of planes shuddering through the sky some 80 meters above ground. Amidst all this, the farmers – Shimamura-San, Fujiko-San and their two sons – continue to grow their 50 varieties of vegetables, supported by feelings of solidarity and committed to a 'slow life' movement and making things oi-shii ("delicious").

Steve Feld
Waking in Nima
sound recording
2012

Everyone experiences waking. But what difference does it make to wake in different places, singly, or repeatedly, and to wake to different sounds? Through years of waking in multiple locales, I am deeply drawn to sonic shifts marking states of sleep, dream, and partial or full consciousness. These provide an unending mix of daily lessons in acoustemology, (acoustic epistemology), in knowing the world sensuously through immersions in local listening.

Waking in my terrace apartment in Nima, an ethnically diverse and class-mixed neighborhood of Accra, Ghana, once-strange sounds have now, after five years, become so familiar that I have the sensation of first opening my ears and eyes to the performance of an electro-acoustic composition in a concert hall. Did I hear that – or did I dream I heard it?

I drift from 5am sleep to Quranic recitation and calls to prayer from close and distant mosques, overlapped by gospel hymns, hellfire preaching, and speaking-in-tongues from close and distant Pentecostal churches. In their layering I hear religious tolerance as acoustic co-existence.

As the sun begins to rise I become aware of the sonic dawn of mosque and church sounds filling out in the surround of roosters, car alarms, voices, street vendors, a distant train. At a moment of emergent conscious awareness I realize that this whole ambient ground is acoustically figured through the presence of songbirds excitedly calling from a tree next to my window.

It's not long before I become aware of my landlord's presence in the flat below mine. He's always up early, sweeping at his doorstep, cleaning his Land Rover, and packing its rear with crates of empty bottles from

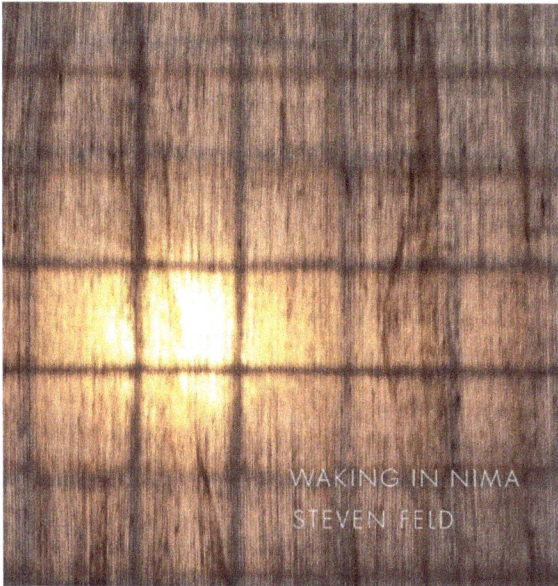

WAKING IN NIMA
STEVEN FELD

his restaurant. Dozing off after my cell phone alarm rings, I know the day is really underway when I hear his engine idle, and the compound's heavy gates swing open.

Waking in Nima is an ambient audio composition that follows my process of waking into acoustic awareness. The sound is mixed from eight real-time tracks recorded 4:30-6:30am from microphones placed in nearby trees and on the roof of my flat. The exhibition excerpt runs 15 minutes; the full CD version is 47 minutes long.
The gallery installation space recalls my spare Nima bedroom, the low-light calm before dawn, the rising sun burning a color beam into the screened window just over my bed. To best experience the acoustics of waking from dreaming, take a pillow, sit or lie on the floor, close your eyes, relax your breath, then enter Nima with headphones.

Catherine Herrera
'Open Doors' Project: The Lost Anthropological Archives of 2012
oral history archive
2012

Catherine Herrera developed her work *Open Doors* "as a tribute to the Ohlone village of Matalan." According to oral history a lodge full of women, children, and men perished in a fire associated with a bounty-hunter in the mid-1800s. This event took place during California's infamous genocidal war against the 'Indians.'

Herrera writes:
`I learned of this painful Matalan incident while tasked with the responsibility of translating a written archive for my Ohlone community. Through this exercise, I experienced my own trauma, recognizing the injustice for my own ancestors and what they endured—a resilience documented in silence, absent from any Western archive. In fact, the impact of historical, intergenerational trauma from cultural genocide has become a contemporary matter, and challenges to justice exist similarly today. In response to these tragic histories of pain and the silencing of Native Americans, and in particular for my own community, I created *Open Doors* as part of my healing process to join together voices, knowledge, and history from both native and non-native communities in a collaborative oral history archive. As a community, *Open Doors* is contemporary anthropology of the Ohlone community, by the community, and, together, we are collaborating in writing a new chapter of our history, telling future generations of how we moved on together to create a new history of collaboration and respect.

Open Doors exhibited in *Audible Observatories* is a small-scale model of the larger *Open Doors Model Project* that draws upon the sacredness of the prayer lodge as a space for healing. The goal of this installation at

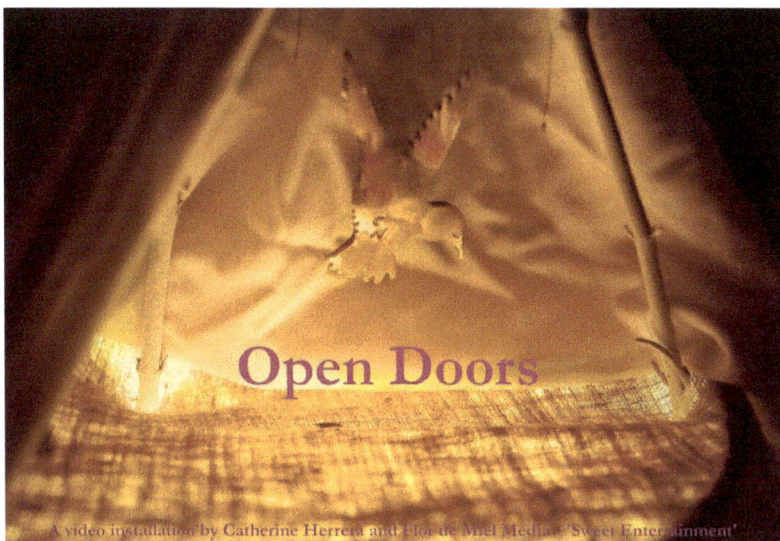

Open Doors

A video installation by Catherine Herrera and Flor de Miel Media 'Sweet Entertainment'

SOMArts is to generate a positive space for a larger audience to gain a renewed understanding of our current historical moment, the role of the archive in reconciling memory and identity, modes of negotiating cultural diversity and understanding, as well demarcate a place for all to positively participate in a communicative space that addresses history, land, politics, and the future. In short, *Open Doors* is about listening and sharing, in a productive way, between communities and cultures.

In creating an iteration of *Open Doors* for *Audible Observatories* I came to question what role I have as a documentary filmmaker in articulating how an oral history archive can better achieve understanding of who we are as the Ohlone today. My goal is to not only comment upon how the ethnographic archive has been used to silence indigenous communities, but also to propose how creating our own archives can enable and empower access to voices, knowledge, and wisdom from our ancestors.

Andrew Irving
Lives of Other Citizens
audio recordings
2012

Imagine if you could enter into other people's heads and find out what they are thinking: the person sitting next to you on the bus; the girl sitting in the corner of the café; the man staring at the pigeons in the park. What would it be like to be able to download and listen to the inner conversations, hopes, fantasies, and worries of the people we see in the city? What daydreams, ideas and opinions would we uncover? What would we learn about human-beings?

This project draws on recent ESRC/Wenner Gren funded research where I filmed and recorded 100+ interior dialogues of strangers I randomly approached in the street and asked to wear a small microphone and narrate the stream of their thoughts while going about their business. This revealed how the people we pass in the street are thinking about a whole range of subjects from the trivial to the tragic. An interactive element constituting a downloadable database of inner-dialogues. The idea being that people can download the dialogues and then walk around the city with someone else's thoughts in their heads.

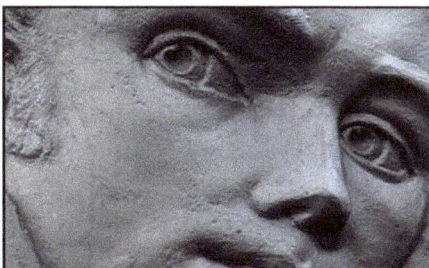

Jenn Karson
Power and Ground
print media & sound
2012

Sound is invisible, sculptural, and malleable, able to take on infinite combinations of textures, timbres, shapes, and forms. In my work with sound I'm interested in the possibilities of its unique ethereal and ephemeral qualities that allow it to move transparently through time and space. What can a deep exploration of our daily soundscapes reveal? How do the temporal and the spatial describe sound?

In my exploration of these questions I consider the textures of recording, scoring, mapping, projection, observation and programming to design installations that are suspicious of the sublime while they navigate the shifting negotiations of natures and cultures.

Power and Ground is a series of sound events documented through mapping, recording, and scoring. The series observes 50 San Francisco sites. The listening methodology used for this project observes the individual actions and interactions of machines, animals, the elements, humans, and money. The sounds are recorded in writing, while maps diagram the location of each sound in relationship to the listener. The scores are time-based documents that indicate when each site recording occurred in relationship to the others. Each score's key creates a system for identifying the type of motion that generated each sound.

SCORE OF SAN FRANCISCO: MACHINES, ELEMENTS, ANIMALS, HUMANS, MONEY

44124   44127   44102   44110

DELIVERY TRUCKS, CHILDREN, FOGHORN, TRAFFIC SIGNAL, MECHANICAL EYES, MP3 PLAYER, BICYCLE, SECURITY ALARM, FLAGS,

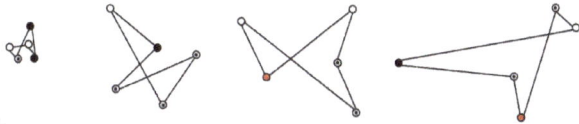

44 and Valencia Canisters of quarters are poured the cement. A motorcycle clops over a sewer lid. Bass booms from a passing car. A street car knocks against its
A dog sniffs at a tuft of grass. A newspaper dispen tra Determined quick footsteps articulat the pavement. Voices between 21 and Crescendo..re Something beeps. Something beeps

44(8)   44(2)   44(2)   44(5)

joining sliding door. The soft paws of a sticky mutt patter again s opened, then slams shut. A woman zips her purse closed. ce A nonpaying customer is asked to leave. She protests. e sidewalk. Shouts escape a kung fu studi

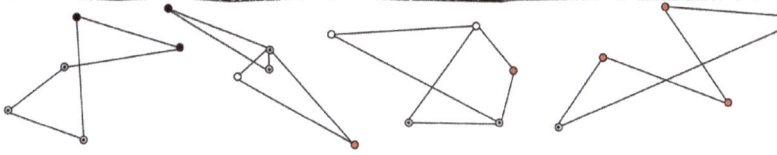

TOURIST BUS   VENDING MACHINE, CELL PHONE, PLASTIC, COINS PAWS, KEYS TIGER, RUBBER, WIND, ALARM, FAMILIES, BUS, SHIP TIDE, ECHO,

FRICTION GENERATES SOUND. TRACKING THE CO-MOTIONS OF THE CITY:

◉ DIGITAL TRANSMISSIONS   ⊕ BIOLOGICAL MOTION   ● MECHANICAL MOTION   ○ GRAVITY & ROTATION

Maryam Kashani
When They Give Their Word, Their Word is Bond
two-channel video installation
2012

The Garden, 9:10 minutes, *The Lighthouse*, 44:00 minutes
A bucolic garden in San Francisco, a small mosque in North Oakland, and storefront windows in San Francisco's Tenderloin are brought together to bring "The Word" to the street. Imam Zaid Shakir is a local African American Muslim scholar who founded the Lighthouse Mosque in North Oakland and is co-founder of Zaytuna College in Berkeley, California. Kashani brings two "performances" together, one a staged portrait where he recites, translates, and provides commentary on his favorite verse in the Qur'an and the second a recording of his khutba (sermon) at the Friday afternoon congregational prayer at the Lighthouse Mosque in Oakland. The Tenderloin is well known amongst Bay Area Muslim populations for its mosques, halal restaurants, markets, and its Arab populations, as well as for its liquor stores, sex work, and drug trade. Recalling the tradition of the street preacher, *When They Give Their Word, Their Word is Bond* mediates a space of the social and the devotional, the spiritual and the practical, and the aspirations of an Islamic future and the realities of Muslim everyday life. This installation is part of Kashani's larger ethnographic project that examines textual practices and genealogies at Zaytuna College and in Bay Area Islam.

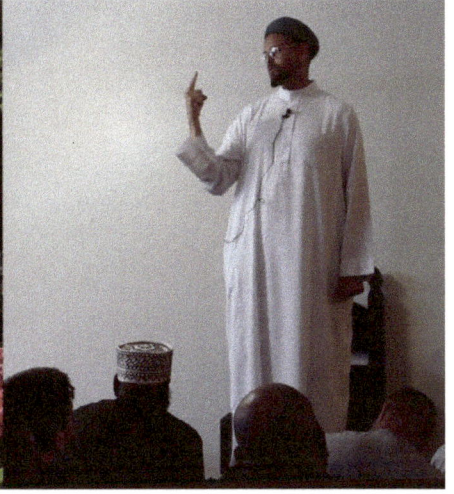

Wolfgang Lehrner
Receiving the World
video installation
2008

Wolfgang Lehrner is a traveller. Portugal, the UK, Bulgaria, Albania,
Turkey, Georgia, USA, Nicaragua, Costa Rica, Panama, Cuba,
Mexico, Jamaica … He calls Vienna his "homebase," from where he
likes to set forth (as often as possible). But it need not necessarily
involve great distances; 15 minutes on his bicycle through the 3rd
district of Vienna – as a "Wettlauf mit/ gegen Zeitzonen" (Race
through/against time zones) – are enough to capture views of the city
with his still camera that might just as well be found in places such as
Berlin, Havana, Moscow, San José and Bucharest.

When he actually arrives somewhere else, the artist may set up his
video camera in a snow flurry, the lens pointing at the edge of a forest.
The caption that is inserted briefly, "Kungsö, Åland Islands, Fin-land,
March 24, 2008, 5:00 pm", raises certain associations with the viewers
that are immediately carried to other places by voices and music coming
from a world receiver radio (which Wolfgang Lehrner simply placed
next to the camera). News from the UK, music with an oriental sound,
a radio feature in German … in between the white noise of channel
scanning. The artist gave to this piece that he presented as a video
installation the title *Receiving the World. Watching local nature while
listening to global culture. Local-Global-Nature-Culture-Time-Place-
Radio-Video-Documents All Around the World*
(Claudia Ehgartner, 2008).

Robert Peterson and Lindsey Reynolds
Radio Transmission Ark
internet-based sound installation
2012

Radio Transmission Ark (RTA) is an Internet-based sound art platform created to encourage explorations in locality and self-representation as well as potentials for broadcast art. Coordinated by artists Lindsey Reynolds and Robert Peterson, *RTA* is a collaborative effort made up of many artists and citizens all of whom are essential to the vitality and resonance of the RTA program.

The first installment of *RTA* took place in the Anacostia neighborhood of Washington DC in January 2012. The Honfleur Gallery hosted us for a month-long residency culminating in a group show that opened on January 13 and evolved until its closure in late February. The openness and accessibility of an Internet platform allowed us to broadcast local stories and music to a global audience. RTA worked with a diverse range of residents and discussed everything from the Underground Railroad and Go-Go music to city planning and the mass of the human brain. We worked closely with young adults from the Hirshhorn Museum's Art Lab and frequently featured their music and stories as a part of our daily broadcasts. Booklets featuring the photographs, hand-drawn maps, and field recordings from the Honfleur residency have been collected by the Smithsonian Anacostia Museum.

A great success the first time around, *Radio Transmission Ark* returned to Anacostia on March 25, 2012 to teach a course with Knowledge Commons: DC. We led a group of public servants, artists, and urban explorers on a tour of the city via the 90 Bus route. The bus became an observatory for examining our surroundings. The ephemera, writings, and photographs from our day-long nano-residency will be published as a small book and redistributed to class members.

Jennifer Schine and Greg Crompton`
Listening to a Sense of Place
film & audio
2012

Using sound as a catalyst and form of ethnography, storytelling, and
expression we invite you to listen to the sounds of the Broughton
Archipelago, an off-the-grid community along the west coast of British
Columbia, Canada. Hear the stories of Billy Proctor, a renowned
pioneer in the community and understand the importance of historical,
contemporary, and environmental listening. This film reveals that
our sense of belonging to place is intimately connected to the act of
listening to it.

Roxanne Varzi
The Whole World is Blind
text & audio
2012

Departing from the idea that seeing is believing and moving toward the theories that Virginia Woolf and Susan Sontag espoused that visuals often mislead if not outright lead to complacency and even engender disaster, this project aims to "see" visuals from recent and ongoing wars without looking. The aim here is not to call out particular places or photographers, but to do the opposite, to somehow neutralize the terror inherent in a war photograph becoming a market commodity, and a work of art. Like Woolf and Sontag in their books, I believe it necessary to describe but not to show war photographs in order to understand and respect the power they hold. Most photographs taken of people in the public sphere are of suffering and most of that suffering is manmade. Leaving a notebook for the audience to comment on allows us to determine how iconic these particular photographs have become in the past few years, if at all.

Do the observers recognize them, even in their most muted form: metaphor? What can we sense about mortality and morality—about war when we allow ourselves to be blinded? When are we forced to listen and imagine? When we stop privileging visuality and heighten our sense of sound? Can it tame the violence of the art? Can blindness lead us to a new kind of vision that would open a space for peace, love and beauty? This sound work loops through a history of the present moment to bring us back to our originary question: is seeing believing? Perhaps the greatest pinnacle of vision resides in blindness. Just as the loudest message is born in silence.

John Wynne
Anspayaxw
sound & photography installation
2011

Anspayaxw (Kispiox) is a small reserve in northern British Columbia, Canada, where I worked with linguist Tyler Peterson and visual artist Denise Hawrysio to record and photograph members of the Gitxsan community. Their native language, Gitxsanimaax, is one of many seriously endangered languages on the west coast of Canada, an area of remarkable but dwindling linguistic diversity. There are roughly 400 'competent' speakers of Gitxsanimaax, but most of these are middle-aged or older and their average age is rising.

Several of the people featured in this installation managed to learn Gitxsanimaax as children despite attending residential schools where its use was forbidden. Such suppression of language by colonizing powers is far from rare: during the 18th and 19th centuries, children caught speaking their native tongue in Welsh schools were forced to wear a block of wood called the Welsh Not, which the wearer would pass on to the next pupil heard speaking the language until, at the end of the day or week, the unfortunate child in possession of it would be struck with it.

Language is a primary repository of culture and history, and once a language is no longer spoken, the rich knowledge it carries is gone forever. The linguistic diversity of the world is under threat: there are currently about 6,000 languages spoken now but it is variously estimated that between 50-90% of these will be gone by the end of this century.

The word Anspayaxw ends with a 'voiceless fricative', a breathy sound characteristic of the language which influenced the way I have worked with the environmental sounds. All the sounds in the piece are derived from the participants' voices and recordings I made in and around Kispiox. Sometimes, these sounds arefiltered, stretched and resonated, but no other sounds have been added.

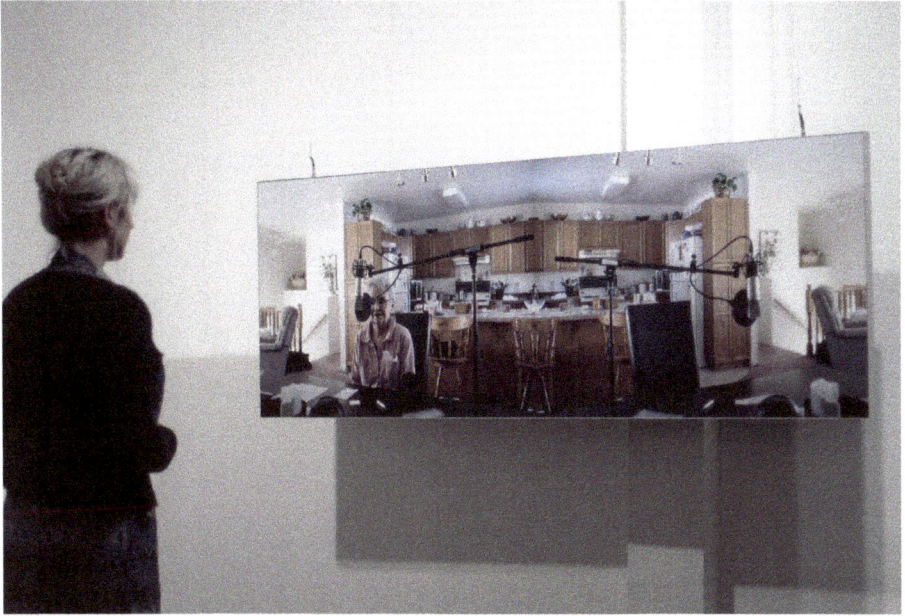

Distributed Exhibition.

The Distributed Exhibition extends the Audible Observatories show beyond the confines of the gallery. This experimental supplement expands out to the streets of San Francisco. Each of the works in the Distributed Exhibition have been placed in publicly accessible locations that resonate with the works themselves. This project carefully layers audio and video works over top everyday experiences of the city. The expanded scope and range of the distributed exhibition allows us to connect with different audiences, creating possibilities for generating new art publics. The diversity of sites—which includes Yerba Buena Gardens, the GLBTQ Cultural Center, SPUR, Siete Potencias Africanas Gallery, and the San Francisco Public Library— reflects the diversity of works in our show. It maps a new layer of possibility over top of San Francisco's dynamic and multi-layered history.

Follow the link below to find the locations of our interactive posters. Participants require a smartphone to view or listen to the works in the Audible Observatories Distributed Exhibition. The works are streamed to the mobile devices via direct internet connection or via an augmented reality application and location specific software.

www.ethnographicterminalia.org

American Anthropological Association
111th annual meetings
San Francisco Hilton (union Square)

SOMArts Cultural Center
934 Brannan Street
San Francisco, CA 94103

Alley Cat Gallery
3036 24th Street
San Francisco, CA 94110

layar

The Distributed Exhibition extends the *Audible Observatories* show beyond the confines of the gallery. This experimental supplement expands out to the streets of San Francisco though a set of nodes and terminals. Each of the works in the Distributed Exhibition have been placed in publicly accessible locations that resonate with the works themselves. This project develops a location specificity which carefully layers audio and video works over top everyday experiences of the city. The expanded scope and range of the distributed exhibition allows us to connect with different audiences, creating possibilities for generating of new critical art publics.

The diversity of sites—which includes Yerba Buena Gardens, the LGBT Community Center, SPUR, Siete Potencias Africanas Gallery, and the San Francisco Public Library—reflects the diversity of works in our show. It maps a new layer of possibility over top of San Francisco's dynamic and multi-layered history.

Process: We worked with each of the artists to find an ideal location for exhibiting their works within San Francisco. Most of the works are not site-specific in the sense that they were created for the location they were exhibited in (Maryam Kashani's "When They Give Their Word, Their Word is Bond" is an exception). The distributed model, however mediates between that kind of site specificity and the locational agnosticism of most works installed in galleries. For example Steve Rosenthal's "San Fran-Man" explores gay men's production of self, through the structural framework of pick-up and dating platforms. After discussion and planning with the artist the curators entered into an agreement with San Franciso's Lesbian, Gay, Bisexual, Transgender Community Center. This location is an important community hub with a broad range of services. The placement of a Distributed Exhibition Terminal at this site introduced the LGBT community to Ethnographic Terminalia and those aware of the main exhibitions to the LGBT community space. On the one hand the distributed exhibition is a kind of treasure hunt spread across the city, on the other it is an enticement to explore the larger theme of the *Audible Observatories* exhibition.

At the core of the distributed exhibition are the terminals. Where the galleries function as hubs and nodes, the terminals extend out from the exhibition to new places. For the *Audible Observatories* exhibition most of the terminals in the distributed exhibition were posters made on an off-set printer. Participants required a smart phone to view or listen to the works. The works were then streamed to the mobile devices via direct internet connection or via an augmented reality application and location specific software.

Mitch Akiyama
I am Standing in a Field
multi-level Audio Recording
2012

I Am Standing in a Field is a reworking, a cover, of Alvin Lucier's iconic 1969 composition, *I Am Sitting in a Room*. In Lucier's piece, the composer enunciates the process by which the work will unfold: he will play a recording of his speech back into the room in which it was captured; over the course of each generation the recording is to become affected by the physical characteristics of the room until all that is left is the sonic articulation of space. Lucier's composition is both a dispassionate investigation into the acoustic properties of built space and an attempt to obscure the artist's presence in the work. Lucier's original transforms space, in this case a simple room, into a laboratory for sonic investigation; *I Am Standing in a Field* does the same, only adopting the eponymous field as its empirical ground zero. In this version, new sonic events insinuate themselves into each playback, each becoming a part of an aural palimpsest. By the twentieth repetition, a car horn captured in take seven has been transformed into an indistinct resonant pulse. *I Am Standing in a Field* is a meditation on the one hundred and twenty year history of field recording, a tradition that has placed great epistemological value in the act of capturing sound out of doors, in the places where things happen, without influence, without interference.

Or so the story goes. But in fact, historically, field recordists have been inveterate tinkerers and tamperers, instructing their subjects on how to perform, on where to stand in relation to the phonograph horn or microphone. They have devised implements like parabolic microphones to isolate particular sounds, thereby creating virtual zones of control, temporary laboratories in the distance. In the spirit of Lucier, in the spirit of the anthropologists and biologists that have used sound recording to gain knowledge of the world, *I Am Standing in a Field* earnestly investigates how sound and space interact. But it is also considers the degree to which sound recording is always caught up in the double mirror of representation.

Thea Costantino, Tim Cunniffe, The Churchlands Choral Society
Siren
audio installation
2012

Siren is an evocative and ephemeral sound installation that temporarily transforms its immediate environment. Disembodied voices travel into a flood of sound and harmony, reaching a frenetic pitch before fading back into stillness and silence.

This work was originally designed for the tower of the Perth Institute of Contemporary in Western Australia. It was activated once per day at nautical sunset and was accompanied by an installation of pulsing light. *Siren* loosely references the maritime symbols of the lighthouse, which guides lost ships away from a hazardous shore, and the siren, whose haunting voice lures sailors to their deaths. *Siren* plays on tensions between drowning and drying, loss and desire, memory and forgetting, consciousness and oblivion.

Siren developed through collaborations between artist Thea Costantino, composer Tim Cunniffe, and an amateur choir, the *Churchlands Choral Society*. The choristers have shared not only their voices but also their experiences in the creation of this work. Costantino developed the libretto based on the choir's thoughts and experiences of loss and recovery, from which Cunniffe constructed *Siren*'s sound world, leading to an ephemeral and poetic reactivation of space and an opportunity for pause and reflection in the night streets.

Lina Dib and Abinadi Meza
Sheaf of Times
field sampling & audio composition
2012

With *Sheaf of Times*, Dib and Meza delve into the foreign world of plants. Using both contact microphones and open-air microphones, they create lofty and minute sound samples. Blurring the boundaries between passively recording sounds (field sampling) and actively making sounds, they focus on plants' materiality, their shapes and textures. This composition is a documentation of interferences, of shockwaves between humans and plants.

Throughout their work, Dib and Meza are attentive to physical manifestations of time. Sound takes time; it can only exist in time. Unlike sight, sound is immersive and simultaneous. Sound physically hits and penetrates. It bundles us with it. It requires and even creates our presence, such that we are not in front of something, but within it. In Jean-Luc Nancy's words, "Sound has no hidden face; it is all in front, in back, and outside inside, inside-out." *Sheaf of Times* is a layering of moments with plants. Using both contact microphones and open-air microphones, Dib and Meza bring together a bundle of interactions, a sheaf of encounters: from lightly touching, to rubbing, to stomping, to caring for and watering.

Steve Rosenthal
San Fran-Man
recorded spoken performance
2012

Today much of our communication occurs virtually and globally;
where once we conversed face-to-face. Can an examination of our
cyber interaction offer up any insight into how we see/represent
ourselves, provide ethnographic specifics dependent on where we are
geographically located, and/or define what a virtual community in
reality is?

Since 2006, my practice has been an evolving exploration of digital-
visual data excavated from online gay community platforms (Gaydar/
GayRomeo/Grindr) then manipulated and re-presented in a miscellany
of forms. For *Audible Observatories* I extend this ongoing investigation
by extracting 'head-line' texts from San Francisco's Gaydar profiles
and reconfigure these silent declarations into poetic form. Forensically
examining the linguistic terminologies employed – seeking out
commonality, repetition, the strange unique and the ordinary,
dissecting the miniature to give rise to an impression of a whole – with
the aim to assemble an 'everyman-portrait', sourced directly from
within, and uniquely particular to San Francisco's gay community
dynamic.

Throughout the summer I have created three such portraits in Berlin,
London, and Zurich for 'Sound Development Cities'. Each assembled
poem was recited through a mega-phone by a gay man, local to each
area, and recorded for re-presentation. I continue this methodology in
the present work to construct the portrait of *San Fran-Man*.

www.ingramcontent.com/pod-product-compliance
Lightning Source LLC
Chambersburg PA
CBHW040138270326
41927CB00020B/3440